Let's Read About...
Rosa Parks

by Courtney Baker
Illustrated by Robert Hunt

SCHOLASTIC INC.   Cartwheel B·O·O·K·S®
New York   Toronto   London   Auckland   Sydney
Mexico City   New Delhi   Hong Kong   Buenos Aires

Rosa Louise McCauley was born on February 4, 1913, in Tuskegee, Alabama.

There were laws that kept black people
and white people apart
when Rosa was growing up.
They were called Segregation Laws.

WHITE

These laws said that black people
and white people could not go
to the same schools.
They could not even drink
from the same water fountains.

COLORED

The laws were not fair to black people. Schools that the black children went to did not have the books they needed.

Rosa's mother wanted her to have
a good education.
She sent Rosa to a special school
in Montgomery, Alabama.

Rosa had to leave home to go
to school.
She had to work to pay
for her education.
She did her best.
Rosa learned an important lesson.
She expected people to treat her well.

Rosa met a man named Raymond Parks
a few years later.

They became friends.
They talked about how much
they disliked segregation.

Rosa and Raymond were soon married.

Raymond belonged to a group
that was trying to change the
Segregation Laws.
Rosa also wanted to change the laws.
She joined the group, too.

Black people had to take a hard test
before they could vote.
The test was not fair.
Rosa helped people pass the test.

Rosa also wanted to help change
another law, too.
This law said that a black person
had to give up his or her seat on a bus
if a white person did not have one.
Rosa thought that this law
was wrong.

Rosa rode the bus every day.
One day, she did something very brave!

When Rosa left work, she was happy
to find a seat on the bus.
The bus driver told Rosa
to give up her seat.
A white man was standing
in the crowded bus.

Rosa was tired of being pushed around because she was black.

"No," she said.

"Well, then I'm going to have to call the police!" the bus driver shouted.

Rosa was not afraid.
She knew she was doing
the right thing.

No one could believe that
Rosa Parks was in jail.
She was such a kind person.
Black people in Montgomery
became angry.

They wanted to make
people understand that
the bus laws were wrong.

The black people had an idea.
They stopped riding
the buses for more
than a year.
Black people in other
Alabama cities stopped
riding buses, too.

Martin Luther King, Jr.,
gave speeches about Rosa
and the Segregation Laws.

Rosa and the group went to court.
They had to make the judge understand
that blacks had the right to sit where
they wanted on the bus.

The case went to the Supreme Court.
This is the highest court
in the United States.
The Supreme Court decided
that Rosa and the others were right.
The laws were changed
in all of the states.

Rosa Parks proved that if you believe in yourself, you can make a difference in the world!